İkinci Yeni
The Turkish Avant-Garde

İkinci Yeni

The Turkish Avant-Garde

❧

Ece Ayhan
İlhan Berk
Edip Cansever
Cemal Süreya
Turgut Uyar

❧

Translated & Edited with an Introduction
by
George Messo

Shearsman Books
Exeter

Published in the United Kingdom in 2009 by
Shearsman Books Ltd
58 Velwell Road
Exeter EX4 4LD

ISBN 978-1-84861-066-8
First Edition

Translations copyright © George Messo, 2009
Introduction copyright © George Messo, 2008
Original poems copyright © Yapı Kredi Kültür Yayıncılık Ticaret

Acknowledgements

Grateful acknowledgment is made to Yapı Kredi Kültür Yayıncılık Ticaret ve
Sanayi for permission to translate work by Ece Ayhan, Edip Cansever, Cemal
Süreya and Turgut Uyar. The translations of İlhan Berk's poems were first
published in *A Leaf about to Fall: Selected Poems* (Salt Publishing, Cambridge,
2006) and are reproduced with minor corrections and revisions. A modified
version of the introduction first appeared in *The Turkish Book Review*. My
special thanks to Dr. Şenol Bezci of Bilkent University, Ankara, and to Mr.
Stephen McLoughlin at The University of Queensland, Brisbane, Australia.

Contents

İkinci Yeni

— *Introduction* —

Cartography of the Turkish Avant-Garde:
Mapping the *İkinci Yeni*

The maps of J.R.R. Tolkien's Middle Earth demonstrate a remarkable fealty to the fictional world they depict. And yet they *are* fictions. They are also astonishing visual manifestations of Tolkien's fetish for facts. Here, I perpetuate my own myth-of-choices, idiosyncratic priorities, shadings and foregroundings, shaped as much by the *idea* of an "İkinci Yeni" and my fealty to a mapping of that idea. In this sense, it too is a fiction, but one that intends its truth.

The story I put together in *İkinci Yeni: The Turkish Avant-Garde* is one of canonical status in Turkey. Simply put, it states: that from roughly the early 1950's until the late 1970's the poets gathered here, collectively and alone, were at the forefront of Turkish poetry's most rapid and dynamic period of innovation and change.[1]

The *İkinci Yeni* (meaning literally, the *Second New*) was an informal group of second-generation Turkish Modernists who emerged in the 1950s, and were active throughout the 50s, 60s and 70s, primarily in Istanbul and Ankara. Though ostensibly a conceptual grouping, the poets shared some distinctive stylistic and poetic concerns, as a well as sharing close friendships, and drew from the work of the French Surrealists and the contemporary European avant-garde. The basic tenets of *İkinci Yeni* poetics were to treat the poem as an object of the deepest subjectivity, to emphasise the self, the individual, and the poetic possibilities of the wounded unconscious.

● ● ●

The phrase "ikinci yeni" was first used by Muzaffer Erdost,[2] in a short essay published in *Son Havadis* on 19 August 1956. Erdost had become increasingly aware, he claimed, of "bir başkalık" (*a difference*) in the poetry being published from 1953 onward, particularly in the Ankara-based *Pazar Postası* (Sunday Post), which Erdost edited.

---

[1] See Orhan Koçak's essay *"Our Master, the Novice": On the Catastrophic Births of Modern Turkish Poetry* in *The South Atlantic Quarterly* 102.2/3 (2003) for a lengthy discussion of this 'innovation and change.'

[2] Muzaffer İlhan Erdost (1932–   ). *İkinci Yeni Yazıları*. Ankara: Onur Yayın-ları, 1997.

The core poets were, according to Erdost, Ece Ayhan, İlhan Berk, Edip Cansever, Sezai Karakoç, Cemal Süreya, Ülkü Tamer, and Turgut Uyar. Despite a profusion of other later voices, these were the most prominent exponents of the new poetics.[3]

For Erdost, the new poetry was "abstract" (soyut), "absurd" and "devoid of meaning" (anlamsız), "introverted" and "obscure" (kapalı), "deformed in form and content" (özde ve biçimde deformasyon); it displayed unique concerns with "individualism" (bireycilik) and "formalism" (biçimcilik); it was a poetry, moreover, that "turned its back on society" (yopluma sırtını dönme) and in this Erdost recognized its central thrust as a revolt, not against tradition *per se* but, against a tradition of poetry-as-public-address. It was, in particular, as Nermin Menemencioğlu later claimed, a "reaction to the brevity and simplicity" of the *Garip* Movement.[4]

The poets of the *Garip* had "sought to eliminate all artifice and convention . . ."[5] In their view, "rhyme and metre, metaphor and simile had been devised to appeal to a succession of elites". It was time for poetry to address the tastes of the growing masses. As Orhan Veli explained in the preface to *Garip*, a book published jointly in 1941 by Veli, Melih Cevdet Anday, and Oktay Rifat:

> "The problem is not to undertake their defence, but to find out what kind of poetry it is that appeals to them, and to give them this poetry. New roads, new means must be found to achieve this end . . .
> The structure must be changed from the very foundations."[6]

The *Garip* poets transformed the notion of what a poem could be in Turkish. And in a profoundly mannered and restrictive cultural milieu, their achievements were little short of revolutionary. The *Garip* movement later became known as the *Birinci Yeni*, or the First New.

While the social optimism of the post-independence years found expression in the *Garip*, for many poets of the early 1950s optimism had

---

[3] Who was and who wasn't an "ikinci yeni" poet is a matter of great importance to some critics. To the names above one might add those of Attila İlhan, İsmet Özel, Özdemir İnce, Süreyya Berfe, and Hilmi Yavuz. And the list could go on. I restrict my selection to work of the five most well-known poets.

[4] *The Penguin Book of Turkish Verse*, edited by Nermin Menemencioğlu & Fahir İz, 1978.

[5] Ibid.

[6] Ibid.

turned to despondency. It was a decade marked by the brutal realpolitik of Adnan Menderes's first freely elected government. The openness of the *Garip*'s democratic rhetoric seemed dangerously exposed in an increasingly closed society, one that oscillated violently between social reform and conservatism, between the promotion of private freedom and public repression.

The linguistic experimentalism of the *İkinci Yeni*, then, in broad terms "reflected a search for aesthetic and philosophical criteria in a society undergoing a new phase of development."[7] Little wonder, at a time when poets were being routinely arrested, tortured and imprisoned, that many sought to explore more ambiguous modes of "abstraction" and "obscurity". The poetry of the *İkinci Yeni* was, in this sense, hermetic, ruminative, subversive—an implosive resistance to the naïve, delusional "open" language of a closed state.

• • •

Unlike those of the *Garip* movement, the poets of the *İkinci Yeni* had no sense of collective self-purpose, no manifesto, and few, except İlhan Berk, warmed to Erdost's early characterization. Berk was often at the center of public debate, and assumed the role of unofficial spokesman for the new poetry. Despite strong friendships among the poets, all (again, with the exception of Berk) came to repudiate their association as a "movement". Edip Cansever was categorical: "Not one of us accepts the *İkinci Yeni* . . . Each of our poetries is different, and not one of us is bound by a shared theory".[8] There were few joint works or collaborations, and no seminal gatherings in anthologies, though several of the poets edited prominent journals and magazines. The critics continued to battle it out. Eser Gürson, an important critic of the 1960s, talked of "poetry rich in possibilities" and acknowledged that "the poetry being written today is in very large measure indebted to the *İkinci Yeni*".[9] In the same period the critic Asım Bezirci sounded off, in a remark clearly aimed at Erdost: "The *İkinci Yeni* is history. Today's Second New is now Secondhand."[10]

• • •

---

[7] Ibid.
[8] In Cansever's *Yaş ve Şiir Üstüne*.
[9] *Edebiyattan Yana*. İstanbul, Yapı Kredi Yayınları, 2001.
[10] *İkinci Yeni Olayı*. Istanbul, Evrensel Kültür Kitaplığı, 1996.

Foremost, and finally, the poems are here to tell of themselves. The poems I select for translation seem purposely at odds with critical pronouncements about the *İkinci Yeni* as a whole, and that, while not entirely coincidental, is the necessary breach through which the poems themselves form spaces for our reception, our own take on their differences, their foreignnesses.

Ece Ayhan wrote fewer poems than any of the other poets here. His dense, darkly lit and obsessive themes of erotic transgression, references to suicide, to physical and sexual abuse broke every conceivable taboo. The unofficial, the unorthodox, the forbidden lay at the heart of his poetic world. His Turkish—flexible, rhythmically taut—as unsettling as his themes, clawed at convention with its elusive unpunctuated syntax, its crooked ambiguities. Ayhan's language takes experimentation to its limits, its melodic tortions sing of the oppressed, of the Pera underworld of Istanbul, of Jews and Greeks and Armenians, pimps and prostitutes, sadistic despots, victims and paedophiles. It was a world never before seen in Turkish verse, a subterranea of the unholy and the damned, of the perverse and alienated, an unrivalled depiction of suffering and survival.

Well known even before the *İkinci Yeni*, İlhan Berk's earlier poems owed much to the realist thrust of the *Garip*: Simple, redolent evocations of Anatolian life and the natural world, for which he was dubbed "the Turkish Walt Whitman". An early collection, *Türkiye Şarkısı* (Song of Turkey, 1953), landed him before the Supreme Chief Justice on a charge of promoting communism. Berk's transition to a more abstract, eclectic and cosmopolitan experimentalism followed shortly after his aquittal. His poem "Saint-Antoine'ın Güvercinleri" (Saint Antoine's Pigeons), first published in *Yenilik* Magazine in 1953, became a pivotal reference for a generation of younger poets. Berk's subsequent work was encyclopedic in range, informed by an eye for intimate, sensual detail. Berk was a celebrant, a magi of the overlooked, conjuring the commonplace into objects of uncommon beauty. He is now the most widely translated Turkish poet in English after Nâzım Hikmet, and undoubtedly the most well-known of the *İkinci Yeni*.

Istanbul is an obsessive presence in poems replete with place names, locations, descriptions. But the Istanbul of the Ottoman divan—the Bosphorus, the rose garden, the mosque and minaret—is passed over for the seamy, opaque shades of Pera, Galata and the narrow, maze-like streets of the decaying European quarter, the red-light zone. Few knew

Istanbul better than Edip Cansever, who lived most of his working life in and around Istanbul's Fatih district, in the precinct of the Grand Bazaar. Cansever was staggeringly prolific and wrote almost every facet of Istanbul life into his poems. His development of the long lyric, his easy-going, democratic rhetoric contrast starkly with Berk's and Ayhan's radical denaturing of the sentence. His human landscapes, surreal urban pastoral, are infused with colloquial, private (and therefore intimately alive) speech, richly idiomatic. Cansever's are poems that *talk*, transcribing the patterns and rhythms of ordinary language into poetic narratives that betray the same nuanced disruptions, about-turns, sudden stops and starts as daily conversations.

Cemal Süreya's 1960s magazine *Papirüs* (Papyrus) was a fulcrum for experimental poetics. Süreya's first book, *Üvercinka* (Pigeon-Tongued, 1958) introduced him as a latter-day troubadour, with his erotically charged language of power and seduction. As with many of the *İkinci Yeni* poets, Süreya prompts a kind of poetic double-take, a re-visioning of his subjects and of the poem itself as object. What masquerades as seduction and conquest belays a more evasive sense of melancholy and lost. The precision of Süreya's metres, the controlled cadences of his music, leave nothing to chance in a world in which accidental sightings, coincidental meetings, take on the greatest significance.

The complexity of Turgut Uyar's verse, its subtle prosody, its visually encoded import, weighs heavily on any translator. His early poems have a kaleidoscopic, dizzying intensity. Punctuation is sparse. Meanings are shaped and arranged cognitively, image on image, into powerful verbal tapestries. His inner world, explored in a language of the deepest subjectivity, is one of isolation and loneliness. Uyar vociferously rejected Erdost's idea of the *İkinci Yeni* and his own part in it. His 1970 collection, *Divan*, masterly reinvents the gazel—the favoured form of the Ottoman court poets—with its strict demands on repetition, metre and rhyme. It was, in a sense, Uyar's final revolt, bringing his formal obsessions full circle back to the syllabic measures of his earliest work.

By the early 1990s only two, Ece Ayhan and İlhan Berk, had outlived the booze and cigarettes. Ayhan died in 2002. Berk, active to the very end, died aged 90 in August 2008. Apart from Edip Cansever, who worked as an antiques dealer, all were sons of the state. Ece Ayhan was a provincial governor. Berk taught in government schools and later as an employee of a state bank. Cemal Süreya was a lifelong civil servant, working first for the Ministry of Finance and then for the Director of the Mint. Turgut Uyar was a commissioned officer in the Armed Forces. From their unassuming, routine working lives they created some of the most imaginatively challenging and sophisticated poetry ever written. Their legacy is the story of Turkish poetry as it happens now, as an act of defiant remaking, broad and various in its practises. The achievements of the *İkinci Yeni* are as relevant now as they ever were.

George Messo
Ankara
August 2009

A Note on Turkish Spelling & Pronunciation

With few exceptions, where Turkish appears in the book I have employed standard Turkish spelling. The exceptions are those words for which well established anglicized forms exist, such as *İstanbul* and *İzmir*, which are commonly written in English with *I* rather than *İ*.

As a guide to pronunciation the following may be useful:

a (*a* in *apple*)

b (as in English)

c (like *j* in *jam*)

ç (*ch* in *chips*)

d (as in English)

e (*e* in *pet*)

f (as in English)

g (*g* in *gate*)

ğ (lengthens a preceding vowel)

h (*h* in *have*)

ı (*i* in *cousin*)

i (*i* in *it*)

j (like *s* in *measure*)

k (*k* in *king*)

l (*l* in *list*)

m (as in English)

n (as in English)

o (*o* in the French *note*)

ö (as in German)

p (as in English)

r (*r* in *rug*)

s (*s* in sit)

ş (*sh* in *ship*)

t (as in English)

u (*u* in *put*)

ü (as in German)

v (as in English)

y (*y* in *yes*)

z (as in English)

İkinci Yeni

— Poetry —

Ece Ayhan

Phaeton

That thing they play on his master's voice gramophones
brittle melancholy of her loneliness
as my sister goes by in a suicidal black phaeton
through Pera's streets of deathly love

My sister toxed-up with gardens and garden flowers
stopping in front of a flower seller's shop with no flowers
with its purple montenegro pistol wrapped in tulle
its oleander photos, Algerian violet in the showcase

I, who've not tried suicide for the last three nights, don't know
if a suicidal black phaeton's rise to heaven together with its horses
could be down to my sister choosing to buy the Algerian violets.

1958

Sword

O seas of vagrancy. O for those whose octopuses were tossed on the shores of unhappiness. My son has opened his wings he is a queen. Wrapped in taffeta. He slowly forgets his sorcerer father was burnt. His winters are spent in Salonica.

He talks to a woman from Mısrâyim. A purple horse his faultless fatigue. Falls asleep among rocks. The sea rises no one knows why. O sunken ships! O silhouettes of exile. I am a weeping half-bred.

Foreboding is an unsayable sword I gird around my waist.

Ocarina

Her thousand years under tar trees
with Mediterranean lips windowless a colicky child
remembering her father as a lake
in the palms of her hands northern moss a lakeful of fish

In an engraved council square
on cold bluish-green Tuesdays the hoffmann rooster
a calamitous clock tower pursued us

A gypsy widow sits on sacks of tea
conniving it seemed to us to turn away her fishy face
in the palm of her hands darkness like chaldean nights

As sun rises over the river
they're burying an ant merchant alive
along with his poor hat wife and sister
silently the first prayer of bankruptcy is ending

Their thousand years under tar trees windowless
Tuesdays a crowd of colicky Mediterranean lipped kids
making obscene gestures
towards unsinkable boats filled metres deep with silk

And the lemon is playing ocarina in its sea dialects
laughing crying screaming lemon-shaped ocarina ocarina.

1956

Jerusalem Rats

In our fourth talk
(where am I?)
in this city before Christ
a trader in ants

He will suffer (a little
death) in the thigh bone
for a sinful ghost
in his palaces

In our fifth talk
(nothing to explain here)
a servant taking arsenic
to his master

In nights of plague
(a yellow moon scissor-snipped)
they trusted
in their deliverance

Since we died when we should
(like chess pawns)
we did not fear lime
or Jerusalem rats
or Jerusalem rats

Such rats as that
such rats as that

1955

The Children's Death Songs

I

mr suburb will one day
lose his thread of course his slides
as he forgets the cock-candy's call

II

the sea is polluted now
voice of my drowned friends
rising

III

today is sunday
my father's at the union
and the earth's closed

IV

no longer enter the cistern
terrible uncle through my eyes
salonica now
is far away.

A Dead Hungarian Acrobat

Later the terrible smiles foreclosed
then I couldn't see anyone
everyone was looking for me
a dead Hungarian acrobat found me found me
monsoon wind was blowing off the sea

1956

The Course of Bad Relations

An acrid tune is sensed on their insides
coloured like their malice
leaving their dead horses
they fled in wooden shoes
old grief of French kings in their eyes

They took our eyes like wine
on the child's lips carried us off
detail of their memories
and songs remained here scores of them
on the beach sea wipes out their giant footprints

1956

Master's Voice

1. The impoverished bird never forgets, it was the year of the burning
   of books

   We saw the grand entry through forty gates
   Of a headless horse and the faded ornament of its rider

   According to dervishes shattered death was returning from the east

   Which is why a stagnant stream divides a city in three

2. The impoverished bird never forgets, boys with dead masters
   They combed each other's hair as they left the sea

   Oh the ripe fresh melon hearts, my young men, Istanbul
   You hide your heart ashamed and smell of rotten flowers

   Above a city something to be read black pigeons are flying

3. The impoverished bird never forgets this golden dialectical law too
   In history so many princes have unknowingly carried their horses

   See on their carved sarcophagi gazels of the master's work

1971

The Unknown Student's Monument

Look here, here, beneath this black marble
If he'd one break more he would have lived
A buried child who'd have had a science oral exam
He was killed in a class on government.

The wrong and common question on state and science was this:
Where does the river Maveraün run into?
From a raised finger in the last row, the only true reply was:
Into the hearts of the pale, downtrodden kid's rebellion.

His old father, second-hand dealer who tied around
His neck a purple embroidered scarf wrote this to stifle his death:
Well, I'd persuaded him he had his toys

Since that day his mother, who wore a guard's coat
And secretly suckled deer foal, a night laundress, wrote down:
Oh they place my son's efforts in his hands.

His friends wove this poem from oleanders:
Never mind no. 128! At the tiny, free boarding school of suicide
In every child's heart there is an older child
On children's holidays the whole class will send you
Birds without envelopes.

1970

Sketched in Hebrew

My legs are long
wherever I go they're long
wherever I go they come and find me
in a cul-de-sac my sister

To sketch a pigeon in this city
to sketch a pigeon's eyes
a pigeon
in the middle ages a pigeon in chalk

The tree's cool shade the length of a wall
I'm sketching a voice
I want everyone to have everyone to have a voice
a voice for pigeon for my sister for the middle ages

Wherever I go they find
me because of my legs always
when sketching another voice
and a holiday town full of flags
in Hebrew.

1956

Mediterranean Windows

Open your windows open them
morning is on the Mediterranean
lower-case musa
forever like this in the sky

I feel pleasure from this white sun
rotten banks and shares
soon earth will be opened
beneath our feet the thousand-fold sea
                          as we drink our tea

He gave out fifteen pence
a fifteen pence newspaper
a woman with her face lit up is calling to us
suddenly

The Mediterranean is created here as we drink our tea
this for our giant lipped
lower-case musa
open your windows open them

1956

The Children's Death Songs II

In streets
deadly oranges
and
indigo clouds
what-
ever the time
a boat loaded with sorrow
on the Mediterranean
deadly
indigo
oranges cloud

The cotton robe
squeaky clean
smells of soap
not well rinsed
the same fruitful girl
choking on tobacco
a fire-colour tattoo on the giants arm

What-
ever the time
the children's death songs
what-
ever the time
it's the children's
ending with an open window
ending in the ash-coloured house.

1956

Poetry's Coastal Voice

Cast into the sea poetry is to me
A star sick for a home it doesn't know

Death is a half-moon sliced by palaces that will burn
Given up to poetry's coastal voice

1970

Canto

A mother's grief was lowered
in bottomless wells two crazy boys in Galata
their legs stretched out on the quay

the passage of seas' lengths and breadths
merges with the sleeping hours of two crazy kids
who'll see nothing of them.

1957

A. Petro

You have a terrible erect smile for sure
a rose-like lip in your bourgeois life

All the streets of your hands a. petro are in love.

1958

Epitafio

Drowned they came from the sea mid afternoon, to hidden blue homes on the wharf of green broadcloth cafes. Spanish fate — .

Bending their heads before their sisters again, as in the morning. So the sisters comb and part their hair down the middle. The deadlock — .

It calls them with shrieks and cries, from a street of playing cards, from the rocks of Malta, with a thousand children's games. The devil's out —
.

They see, and how they laugh so endlessly. But still they cannot come. Their bundles are being packed. They're in a hurry. Rotten — .

I wonder will she appear again, the fat woman who wants the hooks and eyes of her clothes buttoned up, and her sisters, on the mossy hard roads to Africa?

İlhan Berk

The Sea Book

I

Chaws

I read, stretched out, looked at the sail fish.
All day I kept saying this line to myself.
The weather was cloudy, it's cloudy I said.
I went out, walked around, checked on repairs.
I pulled a long face at the workers. A stone had fallen,
a plank out of place: I put them right. A child
dashed an octopus against pebbles. I smiled at the child
then I went and turned on a closed fountain.
A woman asked for a street and I showed the way.
Suddenly I recalled I was going swimming that evening
so I went to change. I saw day creeping away.
I sat down then and worked at my Sea Book.

II

Threewells Street

A whole long day I watched the sea. Great sea.
Storms gathered in. I sat and chiseled out

a skiff. A road lapped its way to the sea,
later going down behind Pazardağ. Barely seen.

A Greek ship off shore was slowing, putting anchor down.
Aganta! I shouted suddenly. The sea echoed back.

The city was water. Water everywhere. Water, water, water.
I threw a fish into the air and the skiff bowed under me.

—The day's shortened, air sharp as a knife! I said.
Then I got up and headed off for Threewells Street.

III

The City

Today I rose early. I woke up the sea.
A man was holding up a squid, showing it off.
I leaned over to look in his eyes, they were sky-blue, round.
He breathed deeply like a heavy labourer.
Three men sat drinking tea and reading the sky.
One was describing the Lodos wind, acting out
the part. "In Bodrum, before Christ, there were only
the Salmakis and Zephyria districts," said another.
I was thinking of the Dorians and Alexander the Great,
of Saint Peter's château and the Chevalier de Naillac.
At six the sun came up and we all dispersed.

IV

Hay

I was on the coast, I suddenly remembered this today.
I climbed up and looked at the city from a hill.

A ruined monastery remained ruined,
I thought of its monks, a little of their women too.

I bent down and smelled a stem of hay, followed by
the long braying of a donkey, a goat melody. I was enraptured.

A man was painting a rusted boat.
I cast him my "hello" into the boat.

Then off I went to draw a sketch of a chimney.
Looking at myself in the evening light: hay from head to toe.

V

Those from Karya

Who are those folk from Karya? Three times I asked. Then
I thought back to yesterday, how I'd been swimming.
I'd seen seaweed. I've wanted to write about it for years
and the sea's depths. Saying this I climbed into bed.
I've a terrible love of my body, my nose, my arms,
my feet; your hairs, my hairs as they rise
on my stomach; my eyelashes and your mouth.
Then my nakedness, my terrible nakedness,
my legs, my groin. That's why I stretch out
my body, why I grow the hairs in my ears.
For my body I say these things. Then? Then
—Who are those Karya folk? I ask, and fill my pipe.

VI

Ecology

I'm learning to name plants. Grasses, flowers.
I take up a laurel. This is wormwood I say.

I'm beginning to inspect from several angles
I tear off a wormwood leaf, then its juice

seeps into my hand. I twist off a branch
from its stem. I count the rings

of a long thin willow branch, then place it
in a stream, alert to the world's opulent greens.

So it is, the whole day I stroll around
then suddenly take up the pen to write.

Novembers

Have you ever seen a city razed to the ground?
So what if I have? Whenever and where it was

stays with me, my acrid history.

Know this

What is time
a November leaf
a child's vacillating mouth
a rose
a left-over, half-drunk glass of water.

Right over there in Topağacı I have my own rose-seller
his face like a closed shop in November,
like the oldest winds.

Me, I'm like a stopped clock in a far-off station
wind flocks around inside.

Know this.

There Have Been Trees I Have Made Friends With

"I filled silence with names." Codified things. I have known the sky's and the trees' infancy. There have been trees I have made friends with. There still are. I didn't understand the Milky Way. Nor numbers. (They behaved as if they had yet to be discovered.) Except for eight (5+3) with whom I became intimate friends. (Who hasn't?) A little with zero too. (It's not been so easy to find zero.) I've heard terrible things about three. Why? I don't know. To know is a number. And I've also met one. You can't think with one. Some numbers are born guilty. One of them is one. I loved stones without asking why. The relation between the pebble's name and its shape has not been proved. I couldn't find a thing on the history of black amber. Fine. Mystery is everything. There are some consonants I couldn't read. (The letter's spirit abounds in consonants. American Indians knew this well.) I accompanied birds. Except for the turtledove, birds know nothing of numbers. Horses, I understood, don't dream in the East. (In Homer horses weep.) I have seen mountains while walking. And thinking as they walked. Recognition impedes reason. *The World is ours!* Said the snails, talking among themselves. I can't say I understand that. Nor that I don't understand it. One should read snails.

As you talk about rivers the rivers themselves are talking, grasses are in their eyes. Time is an illusion. Write this down somewhere. It's not true that spirit has no outward facing view. Jesus' ghost still roams the earth. (I only ask. It's only to question that one writes.) Those who forget their youth stagger in the morning. The rose exists because it is named. Stone got its name when its face was found. (Which is why masons turn stones around and around in their hands.)

I want to return to your eyes. And then . . . There's no such thing as "then." "Then" is outside history.

Yesterday I Wasn't at Home, I Took to the Hills

The sun fathers a cloud in my pocket. I wrote: the stone is blind. Death has no future. Things have only names. And: "A name is a home." (Who was it said that?) Yesterday I wasn't at home, I took to the hills. A gorge looked at us, what it said still lingers in my mind. It was this: we sensed infinity within. Objects are held in time. The tailors' lamplighter Hermusul Heramise's goatskin rose to its feet every spring. Rain cannot not rain. Stone, not fall.

What was I saying, the world has no thoughts. Grasses don't get bored. A pencil thinks it is a tree. The horizon, a hoopoe. I don't know about you, the world is here to be mythologized. It has, therefore, no other end. Transforming into a myth, to be a myth! That's what we call eternity.

Wherever I start, that's where I return. So I'm going. I have work to do on that grand statement, death.

Saint-Antoine's Pigeons

I. Eleni's Hands

One day Eleni's hands come
Everything changes.
First Istanbul steps out of the poem and takes its place
A child laughs
A tree opens into flower.

Before Eleni
When I was barely a child, before I'd got used to coffee and tobacco
Even before I knew mornings or nights
I once looked at night in my hands, in my eyes
Another time morning was all around me.

Eleni comes
I'm looking at the world
That day I realise the world's not as small as it's thought
We're not as unhappy in this world as we think
That day I said we should burn all poems and start again
A new *Brise Marine*
A new *Annabel Lee.*
It's with Eleni we realize
Why this sky rose up, why it came here
With her we understand why the sea packed up and went.

One day Eleni's hands come
For the first time the sea can be seen from a street.

II. Youth

My soul
Do you hear İlhan Berk crossing the bridge?
A sparrow is slowly flying by
A fish with its head through the water is looking around
A leaf is about to fall from the branch.

Lambodis took a bottle from the shelf and opened it.
A cloud stopped in the window
Lambodis went on with his job
Cleaned his hands, sliced cucumbers, tomatoes
Then sat and pondered his youth.

It was in a house
Eleni was eighteen, Ilyadis was twenty-three
Eleni knew songs
You couldn't imagine
    Coffeehouses all over Istanbul
    Pavement cafes indoor cafes
No matter how good the songs
They never could capture Eleni.

In those days Lambodis went everywhere in Istanbul with a cigarette
    in his mouth
Eleni's most beautiful features were her hands, her garlic smelling
mouth
Lambodis wasn't yet a barkeeper
Lambodis wasn't yet anything
In those days they went every Sunday to Saint-Antoine
Eleni's breasts were peeled almonds
Her hands like pigeons
Even then Lambodis' enemies were many
The whole of Istanbul was behind Eleni.

Yes,
Lambodis' youth: a leaf about to fall.
He sat by the window, watched people come and go
Come look he said to me
Look, people are going by
I watch them when I'm bored
And forget all my troubles
We forget all our troubles.

My soul, it's always the same
A man a woman doing the same thing
Soon I'll get up and go to Sirkeci
My sweetheart's leaving on a train
One day the sun won't rise, there'll be no morning,
    we fear one day it will be as if we're not in the world.

This will all come to pass, my soul
One day we'll see Istanbul is beautiful
Thereafter Istanbul is always beautiful
A long long time ago the world was much more beautiful, for example
Those clouds this sky was a place we could reach out and touch
Now they only exist in poems
It all comes down to this, my soul

This world is beautiful
And Gülhane Park is full of trees.

III. Saint-Antoine's Time of Lovemaking

This sky
Is not like this everyday above Saint-Antoine
It's certainly time to make love
Windows are opened first
Ants crawl out of their nest
Mosses stir
Sky draws taut like a drum
A girl stitching in her window is happy for the first time
Homes and coffeehouses facing the sea are happy for the first time
For now Lambodis has nothing to fear
Eleni has nothing to fear
The pigeons will all take flight and no one will know fear
An hour when everything wakes
Love will begin
Everything will stop
A girl's hand stretching out to her dress will stop
Saint-Antoine will rise from his sarcophagus and walk off
    to a place on the coast
With him tombs and holy relics, Jesus himself
    will follow on behind
In everything's place there will be love
Chairs
Windows
Saint-Antoine's ceiling will walk straight to another ceiling
A door straight to another door
Nothing will want to be smaller
You'll see the sky grow large
The sea more blue
This love will go from eye to eye like a dark complexion
Going now to Istanbul along with all the best songs
Now, no matter where, a girls hand, her mouth, grow for this
For this a child clings to its mother's breast

Saint-Antoine's pigeons
Fly for this
The anxiety of order in poetry is for this
This sky can have no other meaning.

IV. Childhood in Fener

Saint-Antoine's childhood
Was spent in Fener

He's just started going to church
The first picture he sees is Jesus' lemon coloured face
The slender legs.
A cloud caught in the window
A child a little older than he is praying
The entire mass of saints suddenly passes before his eyes
The candle falls from his hand.
In those days Antoine's father was a shoemaker in Karaköy
He loved God as he loved his hammer and anvil
In those days it rained everyday in Istanbul

One day he stops in front of Hagia Dikolas' sarcophagus
Who knows how much the sea is missed, he thought
A window opens
They look at the sea
Then he goes home
And explains it all.

Childhood in Fener:
First contact with the sea.

V. Morning

Saint-Antoine recalls a morning
Like mornings which brought with them Ilyadis' songs.
One morning he gathers himself and enters the street
Gazing at shop windows, sky, cinema posters
I am with the new morning for the first time, he says to himself
The first time encountering sea
The first time with poetry.
That day, the whole day, he watches the street
He draws children indoors and talks about improbable things
There is no God, for example, he says
Later together they walk over the bridge
First he says hello to the sea
Then he returns to his place
He sees all the saints have awoken and washed their faces
There is something about this
Saints work like all of us
Some clean windows
Some carry water.

That day there is no evening
Morning never ends.

VI. Eleni Light

One morning Saint-Antoine goes to Iaos Yokios
Night descends on the journey.
Suddenly he remembers Fotini Nermeroğlu
    and goes to Fotini Nermeroğlu's house.
His Holiness Saint-Antoine is here, says Fotini
The whole of Zürefa Street proffers coffee from its windows
The girls hastily cover their breast with their hands
Elpiniki gazes at the stars and everything's in its rightful place
Marvido Apiyos, Eftelya and Hagia Feya, Hagia Dikolas followed by
    Galata Tower, enormous Yüksekkaldırım and Eleni's mouth
    as beautiful as this world all follow on into Fotini's house.
Saint-Antoine looks at the world, "The world's not all that bad,
    Fotini Nermeroglu's not bad at all," he says to himself.
He asks for a Bible
They give him one.
He takes it, crosses out here and there, writes it anew.
Teo Fano, Maneli, Avi Antimos and Kalina step down off a cloud
Salome is on her knees
No, says Antoine at first, there are no longer such things, he says
He raises Salome to her feet
He holds out a Bible to Kalina
From now on, he says, this is the Bible.

Eleni's groin suddenly radiates light
The universe is suddenly sparkling.

VII. Sky

A cloud above Istanbul
White cloud yellow cloud black cloud

5 in the morning
not a sound in Saint-Antoine
what did he do, this man asks
then he answers himself
when we were all asleep
he stole the sky.
What can we do
but hang him.

Ha ha
Ha ha

What do the crowds have to say,
For three days we can't pray
There is no sky

My soul snapped the rope,
the sky is about to fall

What a strange thing this sky
like a handkerchief
we didn't think it would fit in a pocket.

The crowds stir
Who will pull the rope?
Someone says something
calls out

It's nothing

That day there is no evening
Morning never ends.

The Thames

I

Turner sketches the Thames. A northern tributary. Ash smelling.

Was Turner tall? He loved long rivers and the Thames.

Sky like mud.

And Death slowly strolls around as if laying eggs
waving to the Thames from a hill
(as if readying for winter

or for pain).

The Mersey and Humber rivers flow

slowly Thames keels are toyed

a clock strikes three at a crossroads

a cormorant flies in and flies off
a man is selling spermaceti candles
and sticking a stamp on his letter.

It's 1962, I'm in a house in Elsworthy working on a history of a river,
a river as thick as a grammar book and as old as a Genoese sledgehammer
in Galata.

At night I'm out to Piccadilly sitting on a stone
    flushing a pigeon into flight
I break a glass with a black man in a bar and stare
    long and hard at a woman, at a twisting road and
I take up the Thames and go, then perhaps it's another river, the Bosphorus
(so it's the Bosphorus and Asafpasha mansion, its divans and delicate
    curtains
a canary—from the Philippines, yellow, it never sings or else the
canary I'm looking at
    is a window—the interiors of dark rooms, lanterns,
    kitchen hands (mostly Armenian), the men's room, frying
    pans, plates, knifes and forks and lamps, fuses, maces,
    brazier coals, administrators, the little woman, a key, robes
    and
    jackets,
Louis XIV broadcloth shawls and chairs
and a ferry with twin propellers, a round sternpost—and a French
    kitchen top
older than death
in the middle of July).

Perhaps too a fish, a sword fish—obstinate, dumb—and bluefish and mackerel
or else nothing at all.

But I keep a diary in a park and write BOREDOM ten times in a notebook
(a book you bought one morning from Şişane hill from a man whose hands
        spent hours crafting the book
his strange face
that now appears on the full page)
and I stare at a red carnation in the lapel of a passing Englishman
and geraniums.

Here the Thames is like the Danube
thin skinned
and like the timid Golden Horn on the Orthodox shore
and howls in the night in a language I've never heard
with its counter currents and darkness
like a white woman's waking face.

Suddenly I lose her trail at Abbey. She: the Thames. Maybe she's entered a lokanta.

>Cooled some food. Looked out from a window. Listened to a kettle boiling on a stove. Watched its steam rising. Wondering why its water boils. And thought about the days of the week: Monday Tuesday Wednesday Thursday Friday Saturday Sunday. How bored God is on a Sunday. His wearing a cravat. How it rained so slowly that day. How the wind limped around. How the sun withdraws into its room. How she'd closed the curtains and read poems not wanting anyone to see. And then the sun's light.—Sunlight: *I'm here! I'm here!* It said—Perhaps she got lost with a boy from the palace, I say. She washed the threshold of a house. Or greeted T.S. Eliot in Trafalgar Square. And maybe flowed in and out of The Waste Lands. Studied physical education. Practiced gymnastics. Stretched out her arms and legs. Considered her length. Found her width. Worked out the mean. Multiplied. Passed beyond her tributaries. Wrote that down too. Passed onward to Greenwich and Blackwell.

She sat down or thought first of the seas. Absorbed China. And Ceylon, Malta, Jamaica, the Bahamas, Bermuda, Gibraltar, Canada.

Later Australia, New Zealand, India and Africa and the crown republics (*reminders of*

>*botanic exiles*—H.G. Wells) and the British Navy and the Ancient History of the Assyrians and a fur trade centre, Hudson Bay Company and other companies, rail networks and steam ships and two places of exile and a bundle of possessions and Defoe and Fielding's satires.

And then our own: Namik Kemal riding a horse to the
theatre, Sultan
Aziz and his
> garter and Ziya Pasha, behind them prisoners doing hard
> labour and women and men's hats and slavery and bulls
> and horses and The History of Work and John Locke,
> Jesus of Nazareth & the saying: *itiseasierforacameltopass*
> *throughtheeyeofaneedlethanforarichmantoenterthekingdom*
> *ofheaven!* And the 1st and 2nd International and a muddy-
> footed-giant (by the name of Imperialism) and her own
> dirty history

Edwards the I, II and III

The Commonwealth and male sex organs

(the first birds with mammals)

Then she strips off as in the days of Rome. Hangs up her robes.
My 160 miles! She
> says. Looks at a picture on the wall. Her own picture.
> A river like a snake. And twisted. Curling upward
> towards the city. Going down at Limehouse. To the
> West Indies. And stops to look at herself passing St.
> Paul's Cathedral. Coming as far as Bow Church. Then
> stretching out around St. Dunstan. Crossing over

(and)

Strolls around at Customs House. Spins a barrel with a fisherman. They go in and out

> of houses. She seizes hold of a crucifix, a window. They head towards Oxford Street (you know Oxford Street). She bought a banana. Drank a bottle of milk. And said: *It's evening!* And as she stopped two swallows passed each other in flight. First she sent a man on his way to St. Paul's (*I need to go to Hungry. You should ready yourself, I'm passing the Danube!*) At Hyde Park paper fell from her pockets. And there she sat with a Scot.

Then she strikes Blackfriars Bridge and goes on to Bankside.

Crisscrosses up a small rise and gains the centre with a fisherman
passes through stations, winches, the smell of leather. Throws out
> her fishing line
and she comes to a stop beside a piece of Staffordshire porcelain.

II

Is this the morning of 1962? Overcast. Foggy.
A face like Queen Victoria—always gazing off at a distance
and always using her left hand
she never placed her hands on chairs
which is why she always woke at night and changed the water
          of her geraniums
and hash plant—

and morning, always that morning on the road to Henley. Hasty
with small feet
but St. George is peevish and at Rotten Row
she enters a church without taking off her shoes. And never sits

and is jealous of Jesus.

And June is about to fall on the river
and sweet chestnut trees

and a child spins a wheel in a shop and says I haven't slept since last night

and a girl sizes up dantella and tulle to a curtain edge. Her face like paper.

And a man is kneading dough in a bakery and can only read the
   Manifesto in dialect

and there is a watch with a flywheel in the shape of a question mark
   near Hardwich

and the sun is shown with a giant U and the water is 4 + 4

and the watermill on the banks of the Mosel River is as it was in the time
   of the great Karl
a fountain pen
and cotton paper still comes from China to Middle Gardner Street
and to Temple
and to Dombart
Roundtown takes a right at Dombart, takes the night and washing on
   a line.

At St. Petrus again I lose and then re-find the Thames.
And every morning God appears in the form of a glass of water
dresses and goes out into Elsworthy Street looking for a friend
and takes a magnetic needle from the Arabs and gives it to the
        Europeans in 1180
and eyeglasses to Florenza
and uses bonds
lights up London Street in the XV century
makes pocketwatches tick and birds eat grapes
Is carbon an acid? She later asks. If not it's eternal, she says.
Then lifts the lid on Nature's Dialectics
proclaims the immortality of Protein
and turns her head towards the Thames
(Thames: *Where am I?* She thinks)
counting the bridges to herself
moves off towards Greenwich. Sets her watch.
Is detained at Blackwall, seeks out docks, enters and comes out of a canal
crosses to a small island, lingers around houses
(and again thinks of Australia, India, Africa, islands, the Caribbean, Cretan
      oils, broad beans, dill,
                and finally comes right to now)

      God is in the service of the English! She says. And lays down.

And the wind's arm falls.

Letters and Sounds

Şihabüddin Fazullah spoke with thirty two letters and did not have a soul. He believed in letters and earned a living knitting skull caps. It is said he saw every letter in the human face. In the Zeyl he wrote to Cavidan (which hasn't been found), he assigned the letter A to sky; to water: C (water is from Thales); to death: U (Death is a bit U). To fire: Z.

The world was the letter, all forms. Sophocles, who like Pythagoras, did not know how to draw, was also of the letter, as was the cricket, and Mohammed too.

Mohammed (whom we know, spoke with twenty eight letters and had a soul and no bird could ever have flown to where he did) gave ear to sounds. He listened only to them. Everything was sound. Heaven and Hell were sound. A peacock was sound. If Tu Fu rode to Rice Pudding Mountain to graze his horse, it was sound. Which is why he always felt a void between the soul and the forms. And why he seldom wrote. Why should he? Language is lonely. It doesn't speak. The universe is more talkative than us, he said. More leaf-filled. The sun speaks with images. A tree works noisily. So does a stone. Night descends in noise. The universe is sound.

"The alphabet is a peddler."

Askelopis

Askelopis used to walk around with a bird from Ephesus and could see what we couldn't. Objects are like that; not everyone can see them. They love secrecy. Like poets, they too speak in a white language. Reason cannot grasp it. Yet there is nothing that is invisible. Objects don't know this. Why should they? After all, it's not for objects to know. Do fish know the water in which they swim? I recognized the forest without knowing it, and never forgot it*. There's no way of stopping them, once objects turn into words. They envelope the world, then turn into thousands of sentences. In some corner of the world, every morning, a thousand objects wake for this. I came to know the world through sentences. The outer limits of the universe. Language is the only god, that fetus!

(My beloved language, do not conceal those untrodden paths and keep me from seeing them.)

There's nothing more to objects than this. This much Askelopis could not see. Death revealed this to him. (Doesn't philosophy, after all, teach us something about death?)

Would you say objects are lonely?

From now on objects will never feel this kind of loneliness again.

I promise.

Edip Cansever

Eyes

As if nothing can arouse
Our inner silence
Not talk nor words nothing
Eyes bring forth eyes!

Nothing else unites us but this
A leaf's touching another leaf
So close, so compliant
Hands bring forth hands!
I say, in our age love is a kind of conflict
Let us join to set two single shadows free.

Bedu

Through the desolate, dull, brown city of my eyes
White-necked camels pass with their tired drivers
Days on end as if on the verge of understanding
They look unceasingly to a place far in the distance
Ask if they have seen, as clearly as a fairy tale, the things they saw
Through the desolate, dull, brown city of my eyes.

Towards an unknown place; not day, not death
They only look
A bedu stands among white thorns
Among gods and suns and mirages
Not even a fire, a plant, not even a prayer
In the desolate, dull, brown city of my eyes.

What he looks for, who knows, perhaps only water enough to quench
        a thirst
No halting place, no rest
If they come he will not hear the white-necked camels
Even as their tired drivers collapse in front of him
Like the coldest desert bird dying again
Into the world's monotonous colour.

Argument

His feet are pointed as he treads on hard stones
The women have breasts—let's drink whisky or beer
See, there are tables that are not alive
Just like that a table in amongst them
Tonight to the women tell Mike and Jim.

Mike doesn't like women, we'll drop him at the coffeehouse whatever
He'll play cards a while and open up to the oceans
See, there are islands that are not alive
Just like that an island in amongst them
You know us right—he winks—to the women.

His feet are pointed as the sky beats down on roofs
This argument, this unwavering argument
See, there are people who are not alive
Is it you Mike, or else you Jim
Tonight, let's not worry women, he sighs.

Rooster and Stairs

Upstairs is upstairs, downstairs is a little downstairs
The rooster and stairs are in the middle
Precious rooster! He bleeds into colour on the stair
The red of a whistle makes the child more a child
A ten fathom thread calls out to my mother
I look down to see the water bucket;
As many fish as I think there are fish.

Gravitational Carnation

Do you know you live a little in me
Yet it's possible to be beautiful with you
We're drinking rakı, say, as if a carnation were falling inside us
A tree works away like clockwork beside us
My mind and body in tatters.

You're hooked on that carnation, I take it and give it to you
You too give it to someone else more beautiful
Isn't there that someone? Who passes it on again
And in doing the carnation goes from hand to hand.

So you can see we foster this love
I mention you, give warmth, but that's not it
Look how like seven colours cut into white
We coalesce without a sound.

Dwarfs

Nights won't pass, heavy they linger
Ill-tempered, seep through windows lunatic
And the dwarfs, they're singing in the kitchen
Tearing at their tongues with forks
Their songs shudder with blood and sinew.

Inside me I flog my face, my terrible face
There I laugh at pain
I don't even laugh at pain
Like a many-armed sea monster
I drive it mad with lust
The dwarfs are singing in the kitchen.

Let's drink o dwarfs, let's drink
We have time on our hands
For new pains not yet born.

Cross-Section

The arcade with its roses its gladioli and its pimps
That irascible thoroughfare
That's where I hide
Weary leaving the excavation
Dream fossils in my eyes.

I would surmount love if madness did not threaten
If nothing threatened
Bleeding so as to know death
A lady-boy's mouth
Stabbed to a convex mirror.

Blood, the source of everything, blood . . .

Oh Yeah Now That's a Table

A man filled with life's joy
Placed his keys on the table
Put down flowers in a copper bowl
Put down his milk, his eggs
Placed light coming from the window there
Sound of a bicycle, sound of a spinning wheel
He placed there the softness of weather and bread

On the table the man
Put things that occurred in his mind
Whatever he wanted to do in life
He placed it there
Who he loved, who he didn't love

The man put them too on the table
Three times three equals nine
The man placed nine on the table
He was next to the window next to the sky
He reached out placed infinity on the table
For days he'd wanted to drink a beer
He put the pouring of beer onto the table
He put down his sleep his wakefulness
Placed there his fullness his hunger

Oh yeah now that's a table
Never once complained about the load
Once or twice it shook then stopped
That man kept putting things on.

Triplets

I
Smile! See its immortal reply
Here you have
Lamps, glasses, flower-filled autumn carafes

II
The day's first hours
I know well these are the day's first hours
Well, what then is this morning erasure

III
I am in the words and songs
Never sung in any tongue
Never written in any language.

IV
Why does your waiting in the station buffet come back to me
It grew cold—the last days of November—
It will snow, your forgottenness will be brilliant white.

V
A boat passes, a silent boat
Yet full of passengers inside
When entered there is no one—apart from waves—

VI
It rained all day
Or else a year's worth in a day
It drenched the day

VII
What is loneliness—ask yourself first—
One early morning when you see the glow
Of a single dewdrop on a wildflower

VIII
You have no shadow, no footprints
Why is that? No sufferings dwell in you
No happiness, no unhappiness.

A Paper Rose in Her Collar

A paper rose in her collar
The faded velvet hat cocked to one side
Her eyes, her old eyes
A thousand miles away from her
Now a pair of wide-open ships lanterns
A dense winter mid-afternoon outside.

A dense winter mid-afternoon outside
Soiled snow clouds, wind
The lokanta like a dejected theatre placard
—O these lonely mid-afternoons!—
Always pulling her short skirt straight
And here
Another poverty added to poverty
She eyes me from head to toe. Well,
Why shouldn't I offer her a cigarette
Or should I first send a drink to her table
—O these lonely mid-afternoons!—
Best if I get up and go to her

> Say hello from the heart,
> With love, full of warmth

Steal my glance away from her dirty knees
And her legs full of bruises
Should I reckon in
Her shapeless narrow forehead
And shouldn't I care at all
About the mole on her chin
—O how the Christmas bells chime outside
In some church in Taksim or in Tarlabaşı—
Could I if I want to

Yes, really, so what
If I say hello to her

Should I first take her to dinner
Or she'd suddenly take offence
Salad, steak, wine
Then apple pie, coffee
We could slip outside later, walk a little
Why not—why ever not—spend the night together
(A few chairs in her room
lots of pictures stuck to a broken mirror
and a brass bedstead
walls dropping their plaster)
should I take her out, away from this winter mid-afternoon

But first before anything
I should say hello.

And in the morning
When the first rays of light fall into the room
Sketching the last scene of this "desperate play"
(Awake before me, she is making tea
a rickety table
a carafe—its bottom yellow stained—
But somehow when our eyes meet
She turns off towards the kitchen
Dragging a pair of misshapen slippers
—O these squalid mornings!—
And turning constantly
The silver ring on her finger)

Yes, while there's still time
I should say hello.

82

She got up and left then pausing a little
Gave me back the dream I'd had
She left
With her paper rose and velvet hat

     O how the Christmas bells chime outside
     In the trembling winter mid-afternoon and in the solitude.

Three Women

Three women enter a garden—what will happen now
The third's eyes filled with tears—what will happen now
Three candles in their hands—what will happen now
Three of them lit their candles—what will happen now

All three, like the winter of daylight
Three, a sheaf of earth made from light
The three, a garden furnished with pain
An acacia, a marble table, and a chair.

It Was the Jazz Season

It was the jazz season—what else was it—
Saxophones in the city's broken mirrors
And tramways—in the brass section—
Polished and sunned-up
It was the jazz season, starched stiff collars
And straw hats
Would dampen in closed salons
In stations where you cannot live by breathing
At tram stops where you cannot go by going
And in those ghetto bars—dilapidated—
Quite quite
Sad as sad
It was awaited without resistance.

It was the jazz season
Maybe it was a newspaper wrapping rotten apples
A season when giant ships
Stood open mouthed
With yearning in those viscid streams
And withered oranges—blood oranges—
That came shuddering back to life in stone buildings
- When eyes were suckled between pauses—
such a season it was, even picture cards
were charming corpses lined up in rooms.

It was also early summer trumpets
Catching and escaping
Countless pigeons
Purple-pink pigeons. I mean
Everything was kind of like a child, palaces, even temples
And clock towers
Children were ceremonies, displays
Pavements, mourning clothes
And perhaps too an unstable, hesitant

Whirlwind inside a storm
—In all the music topographies
At least, its name was known—
It was the jazz season, one of the seasons
A sunless deck—freed of its ship—
As if it remained alone
Leaving the taste of loneliness
It would slide between tongue and palate, and go.

The cover over our eyes was like downy sheet
Mid-afternoon was quivering on the tables
Three or four people agreed on the same thing
A silent accord
What did it matter, a "do" too far, three "me"s missing
Everything, everything, but everything
For example, King Henry's pallid face
And Prince Hamlet's
—That is, any day in history—
On a crumbling plaster wall
Quickly became identical to far off figures.
And a squirrel and a frail Jew
Became inseparable
Like the Jew's stooping shoulder
Then the evening crowds with their indefinite fantasies
Were ironed together
In one swift jerk of the face a thousand drinks were drunk
- It was a sticker whichever way you look
Early summer
When it rained a little
In artificial colours
Permeating deep into our nature—

It was the jazz season—one of the seasons—
Loneliness was an infectious virus

That filled time here and there
Rolls Royces and wedding dresses
And flowers, the most outrageous types
Like gladioli and roses
Very few carnations
Each equally adorned with the other
Was it possible, but it happened
A charming, long-moustached criminal
Dropped his watch chain into infinity
—Wherever he found infinity—
Whose name was unknown in police files
And you could not be more surprised by everything there
For example
If Larousse's encyclopedias came to life a little
Spread into the surroundings
For us the most conciliatory
For us the most desolate images.

Buses turned back from their routes
—It was a movement, what more was it—
No one climbed on those buses
But nobody
Everyone gathered at bus stops waiting
Did you say Sunday
No matter it was Monday
Was it early summer
It might even have been autumn
Because every question
Was to casually gnaw an apple
What was the reply
Nothing but the question
Agreement too
Was a holy book
Between a widow and an imam.

It was the jazz season—only a measure—
And it was strange, even remembering
Was remembering
Borrowing from the future
And that was a cause of happiness
A reason for unhappiness
As if a perfectly unique garden
From the peak of nonexistence
Had come down piece by piece.

Because it was the jazz season—what more was it.—

Awakening

I'm waking up waking up
Four walls
Yes, four walls
So what's behind the wall

—what's behind the wall
—a child, another child, children . . .
—what's behind the wall
—a woman, Catholic, removing her mourning clothes
—what's behind the wall
—an old man, relaxing in the sun
—what's behind the wall
—a ship, a passenger ship, lights inside
—behind the wall . . .
—a lawnmower, a pool
—behind the wall, the wall . . .
—fishermen back from hunting, fish coloured "sea-like"
—what's behind the wall
—whatever, a theme park as big as a snowball
—behind the wall . . .
—because, as you see, now, later . . .
—behind the wall, the wall . . .
—white whiteness
—what's behind the wall
—a song, full of meaning
—what's behind the wall
—an angel, three-winged
—behind the wall . . .
—What else do you expect
   a washed and purified sky
   a bubble-fluffy world

Four walls?
Yes, four walls.

For 15th March 1985

—Tell me the name of a flower you've never seen
—Not one, not a few, but thousands
   a whole life I cared for it grew it
   gave life to it in my eyes

—Tell me like a secret the name of a flower
—Summer is here, so if not violet what?

First Epistle to Hilmi Bey of Monastir

See this rain, this balcony, me
This begonia, aloneness
These drops of water, on my forehead, on my arms
This city born of my death
I'm flowing nowhere, only oozing into myself
By me I mean an enormous hole
In the chair, in the mirror's reflection
A hole! In the sofa, the kitchen, my bed
As if I'm looking at life upside down
Often I find my own way around it. For instance
A season comes to a close in one or two hours
Good
Is it Monday today? The state of the door and window
Says it's Tuesday.

The huge living room clock I sold
There isn't so much as a scrap of time
A clock could measure
I'm like those insects that don't know where they're going
To some crevice, to some hollowed out life
What use is a clock
I'm always going out on the balcony
Roads roads roads as if that's how I get about
Taking in the first colour of a neighbourhood
In Ümraniye for example I'm in a tea garden
Sometimes
A road from one memory to the next
And
A garden swinging from one memory to another
Whichever leaf I tear off its last memory is left in my palm
Good.

Shall we drink a coffee in Yeniköy, I said this morning
This morning this morning
No one cared less—was it Monday—
I'd just crept from my hole, my begonia among roses
How's that?
Well, like roses among roses
And a seagull on the balcony railing. I said
The sea must be around here somewhere
Not a sound inside the house
The sea must be around here somewhere
Not a sound
As if all the teahouses in the world were closed
And I'm a street that goes down from sky to hilltops
Or I'm river, me
If the sea
Is around here . . .
Never mind only two days left—seagull—
On the balcony
Then the sea died, the seagull too
Good good.

It's all like trying to hold water
The days—when I remember you—
The sudden noise of a tram going from Kurtuluş to Taksim
A blue spark of electric beneath wires
As if it's snowing constantly, we're in Tepebaşi
Snow scrunching passed beneath my feet
Of course we're in Gümüşsuyu, we're in a Russian lokanta
—How strange, we're always everywhere together—
We've drunk wine and we're cold
The world outside is erased
The two of us two of us two of us
The two of us over and again like that
Then everything transforms into a photograph
Somehow
A brown photograph absorbing yellow and scared of purple
Really, if I stay here I should put something on
Not that I'm cold
The quivering voice of a girl who says
"I have everyone in me" falls into my lap
My lips are bruise-blue today.

We're good here we're very good here
Here we're all forty years old
The four of us are one person, so
Should one of us fall asleep, or so on
We wait for her so as to be one person
Yes yes, I'm not mistaken
When there are one or two people I can make mistakes
It's true
To make mistakes is like seeing everything for the first time again
Stained glass on the wall, the begonia
Begonia, stained glass
Kurtuluş and Asmalımescit intermingling
A point of separation between the tram's stopping and not stopping
Perhaps it smells a little of carnations
I'm a freshly picked bunch of carnations
My hair is cold and long.

What was I saying? Rain, yes
I'm not cold I've got goose pimples that's all
Like a cat wrestling to get out of its skin
But wait
The doorbell ringing, no, the telephone
Telephone door telephone
Or else both at once
Or else
Neither telephone nor door
The sound of thunder at least
But no
I didn't hear a sound
Was it the soft sound a snowball makes
When it's rolled to make it big perhaps
Two sounds within a sound
And why not
As it did a moment ago
Someone rose from on top of me—nooooooo!
Not like that, it was a shadow that's all
A traveling shadow changing place
From the garden walnut tree
Dragging itself inside.

Second Epistle to Hilmi Bey of Monastir

We're at the water's edge of your silence today
No matter how lovingly we talk—and we're talking—
When we come face to face we're afraid Hilmi Bey
We're afraid
As if our eyes were each other's rival—isn't it so—
And it's like we're going down a hill
Always from one hill to another
—To where?
—I don't know
The sound of alcohol in our hands, in our hair
The sound of alcohol
In our mountains, our inner seas
And days pressed one inside the other as slowly they unfold

The decanter is stuck in its place
The windows are confused
The curtains are as long as a distant road
And the balcony
On its own lips now
A frozen peacock
Maybe a statue of a peacock
How strange
And just now downstairs a brass band went past
I wanted to ask you
A brass band leader's sorrow is what Hilmi Bey
A brass band leader's sleep
Is what kind of sleep Hilmi Bey
How awful
Summer passed with a flower in my hand

And today
We all sat around the table again
And played cards Hilmi Bey—everyday we play—
Undressed, just in our dressing gowns—you know—
The room was roasting—the ruby coloured Chinese stove—
Seniha putting on her corset, the Jewish mademoiselle
Almost naked—sweating sweating sweating—
And Cemal is watching us from a corner
Watching as if he were not watching
Lingering as if not lingering
That's what I don't understand
Yesterday he cut his lip in the market
He was fooling around with a red fish
Suddenly he kissed it—who knows why—
And as he did he cut his lip
The fish was red, the blood too
And the fish swam off—I saw it—
Away from his lips
And stopped like Cemal a little further away

Lingering as if not lingering
He didn't cry, didn't say a thing
The man's a riddle unto himself
Except he asked, and that's why I'm asking you
Are angels female Hilmi Bey
He thinks they are
But me . . .
If that's so who am I
A fake flower in my hand.

My name is Cemile, I love my name
A name is a person's childhood
Cemal is only Cemal for now—yes, that's right—
Mine is a memory—Cemile—
Cemal-Cemile: sound of a freshly shooting lettuce
Two crushed cherries
And at night
Night is about to find its hammock to swing from
Finds it

The waters were violet-petalled Hilmi Bey
There was a large lampshade on the ceiling
I'm a little tired—we drank the entire day—
We all drank
Cemal never left his room
We played tangos one after the other
Old tangos—what was it with nineteen fifteen
When I looked out of the window
None of them had died
There's no such thing as death Hilmi Bey
Was there ever?—
Something dripped dripped from my face
My insides were violet-petalled Hilmi Bey
This childhood was something like the sky
Going nowhere.

For some reason as Cemal hides in his room
Undresses the Jewish mademoiselle keeps undressing
Like a woman full of desire
Esther, I say, Esther
She smiles lightly
As if to someone else smiling back
Have you seen when two people are kissing
Hilmi Bey
That's exactly how it is
Then she dresses quickly, goes outside
Suddenly we're three people
Like a newly bitten apple
Our green side glistens in its own light
A coldness inside me
Outside me, a begonia.

It's perfectly dark outside
We've drunk our raki—the three of us—
Cemal doesn't leave his room
Soon Esther will come
She'll collapse in the chair, light a cigarette
Again the four of us will be like a cross
A huge cross inside a house
Not holy but dirty
Not exuberant, but worn out
Joyfully we draw it to ourselves.

The Metal Shop

I cast an eye at the sea
The fish are singing ring-a-ding.
This is a worn shoe I say.
This is a water-logged cheese I say
That's a boiled potato in your hand.
This is human intuition
This is human reason
This is the rule of law
Like strawberry's genesis into strawberry.

So this is reality and you know reality
This hammered peg
This kneaded bread
This knowledge of love and shame and man
This feeling, this thinking, this human burden
Both inside and outside this group
This is your station, this is work in nature
This dumb flower
This ignorant tree
This sheer foresight
This water, this river, this wind
This stone, this cloud, this air
This known, this unknown
This time before Christ, this time after Christ.

Here this latest man;
The stacked boxes
The dented tins
The metal shop.

A Glass of Linden Tea

As you push the glass of linden tea aside
And lift your head from wet-hair scents
Your eyes
Are the insides of a ripe apricot in you.

Last night your shadow spread across the ground
Lies on top of tonight's shadow
A handful of sunflowers in your pocket
Is back with us here somehow.

Your eyelashes open and close
As they live in the brief pause happiness bestows
I don't know, will you take offence if I say:
Your beauty's source is a long-forgotten ugliness.

Cemal Süreya

Striptease

However many notes
Do re mi fa sol la si
That's how many
Clothes she wears

Her shirt is fa
Her bra is sol
Her high-heels la
Her hat si

She adored them
Like her own body

Slowly softly she dresses
At home in the morning
First do, then in order

            re
          mi
        fa
      sol
    la
And lastly her hat si

She bursts forth like a flower
From her front door

But, when tonight on stage
The music starts you'll see
Everything suddenly speeds up
Her nostrils begin
To open and close

Not far away the piano
Accompanies her

With a terrible fury
She throws off
What's on:
Take it si
            And la
                    sol
                        fa
                            mi
                                re
                                    dooooo!

Photograph

Three people at the stop
Man woman and child

The man's hands are in his pockets
The woman is holding the child

The man is sad
Sad as a melancholy song

The woman is beautiful
Beautiful as beautiful memories

The child
Sad as beautiful memories
Beautiful melancholy songs

Through Glass

Leaving the bar
I looked back
through the glass
to the place I'd just sat.

I'd left my packet
of cigarettes on the table.
In the chair
my own blank space sitting
exactly like me.

A hand on his brow
just like me.
But
is he even more melancholy?
When he sits
does his hump stick out
that little more?

Is he more like
my father?

I'm one year older than my father
and the wind
as if in some ceremony
keeps tugging
at my raincoat.

The 8:10 Ferry

Do you know what's in your voice
There's a garden's centre
      Blue silk winter flower
      You go upstairs
      To smoke a cigarette

Do you know what's in your voice
There's a sleepless Turkish
      You're not happy with your job
      You don't love this town
      A man folds his newspaper

Do you know what's in your voice
There are old kisses
      The bathroom's stained glass
      Your temporary absence
      There are school songs

Do you know what's in your voice
There's the disarray of a house
      Sometimes you take a hand to your head
      Your loneliness scattered there in the wind
      You're sorting it out.

Do you know what's in your voice
There are words you didn't say
      The tiniest things perhaps
      But at this time of day
      They stand like a monument

Do you know what's in your voice
There are words you cannot say.

For Eray Canberk

Dear Eray
Translates his silence
For the folks
In the sea restaurant.

Short

Life is short,
The birds are flying.

To the Milky Way, Via 1994

I've lived, my God,
Poorly and rashly,
But in another life,
If there were such a life,
Would I have written poems,
I don't know.

But women, my God,
How I've loved them,
The next time
If I come back to earth
As a woman,
I'll be a lesbian.

Picture

A war: the battle of Otlukbeli*
A blue: Spartacus
A question: why Spartacus
A bird: where are you gong, bird
A flower: I don't know the flower
A lake: uncertain

A document: from a notary
Surely a notary from the capital
A poet: Ahmed Arif
Collects the mountain's winds
And gives them out early to children
A child: thin-nosed

O thin-nosed child from the South
Ask whatever it is you'll ask
A musical instrument: the phaeton
A drink: rakı not vodka
A gun: loaded of course
A newsflash: my death is near

A signature: unreadable

* *Translator's note:* The Battle of Otlukbeli was fought in 1473 between
Fatih Sultan Mehmet (the Conqueror) and Uzun Hasan (Tall Hasan) of the
Akkoyunlu Hükümdarı (White Sheep Tribe). The town of Otlukbeli is in the
province of Erzincan in Eastern Anatolia.

Song of the Executioner

A hundred and fifty years
After the bourgeois revolution
A Parisian lawyer Monsieur Guillotine
Reads of suicides in the morning paper
With tears in his eyes.

Senior Bullet. Spain.
Your glance can stray
Dragged off by a cloud
Unless of course like Lorca
You were blindfolded too.

And what's to be said
Of Mister Electric Chair
Credit payments to one side
A better symbol of America
Than William James

The spurting blood is a salute
To Cain to Ezra Pound
In brackets to Raskolnikov
The head not realizing
Goes on giving orders to the feet
But Herr Hatchet's job is done

Citizen condemned to death
If you can scrape your breath
When the chair is pulled from under you
You will live that little longer
For the death proffered by Rope
Effendi is a death of polite delay.

Repute

My breath is a red bird
In your hair's auburn skies
I take you in my arms
And your legs grow indescribably long

My breath becomes a red horse
I can tell from my burnt face
We're poor and our nights are short
We should make love galloping.

1957

Rose

I weep at the core of the rose
As I die each night in the open road
Knowing nothing ahead or behind
Sensing in darkness the dimming
Of your eyes that keep me alive

I take your hands, loving them until dawn
Your hands are white forever white forever white
Hands so white that I'm afraid
A train is at the station a while
Sometimes I'm a man who can't find the station

I take the rose, rubbing it on my face
Fallen somehow over the street
And here I'm left high and dry
The blood, the uproar, the instrument
And on the end of the pipe a newly born gypsy

1954

Two Hearts

The shortest path between two hearts:
Two arms
Reaching out to each other and now and then
With only the fingertips touching.

I'm running to where the stairs are,
Waiting is time's conquest of the body;
I came very early and cannot find you,
As if it was a rehearsal for something.

Birds are gathering and migrating
I wish it were just for this I loved you.

Pheasant Face

The pheasant's face is an atmospheric event
I learnt this by chance from a writer-hunter:
Wild ducks take turns to beat their wings
On water so that it doesn't freeze over.

And so here's your Beşiktaş with its buoy,
Throwing back a confused century;
My god was it you who created this long
Anatolia in your childhood days?

The screenwriter and I are sitting on a beach
I wish it were just for this I loved you.

At Afyon Station

You recall that little girl at Afyon station
Who took off her shoes as she boarded the train;
Think of the Varto earthquake, a box of milk powder
And a bra sent as aid from the West.

The man whitewashed his house with milk powder,
His wife kept the bra not knowing what it was for;
She thought to use it for earmuffs in winter;
My god, was that really in your childhood days?

A host of people sitting on thresholds
I wish it were just for this I loved you.

Enamel

A gold enamel watch,
A golden watch chain and a medallion
A rose diamond lucky charm,
Twelve miskal pearls.

I pressed inside
Your bead and medallion
Stirring the depth of our eyes
Like the mist of a far mountain road.

An unfinished silver box on your chest of drawers
I wish it were just for this I loved you.

18th December

In that salon 18 December 1985
Who could have predicted?
You, archaeologists, fortune tellers,
Let the years pass like years.

Could we forget Louis XVI,
Evening of 14 July 1789,
Louis, who wrote in his notebook:
"Today nothing at all noteworthy . . ."

I found a tiny poem called "prophecy"
I wish it were just for this I loved you.

A Flower

Some place, over there, stands a flower
Opened up as if to correct a mistake;
Comes all the way to my mouth's edge
To stay and talk.

In the wide open a white skinned ship
Its decks all forest from stern to bow
I grasped my flower pressed it to me here
Pressed what was my loneliness.

A man alone strides through a blue train
I wish it were just for this I loved you.

Night Flowers

I'm afraid of night flowers,
No, afraid of flowers at night!
Concealing themselves, each phone call you make
To me is a requiem to the shot messenger.

The shortest path between two hearts:
Two arms
Reaching out to each other and now and then
With only the fingertips touching.

Time is eternity's spring
I wish it were just for this I loved you.

I Threw a Tab-End into the Sea

Now we share a pigeon's flight
On the famous blue roads of the sky
With long-haired big-breasted women
A Mediterranean city may arise
If now we tear apart
A pigeon's heart

Time it is now for you to love
Time to stand beside her, to hold her hand
By which hand my love which hand
In one your virginity strange cranky
In the other a nubile radiance
In yet another a boundless freedom
And with one hand you break bread
For workers who toil in dust and smoke
From morning to night.

So we were, more or less like this
If a cloud had passed we'd see it
Or if a minaret was overjoyed we'd see it
If a man was forever fighting poverty, we'd see him
Whenever we throw a tab-end into the sea
For liberty, peace, for love
It glows on till dawn.

1954

Wave

They cut the cloud, cloud into three
My blood spilt out, cloud into three
Two sailors filched from Van Gogh
And a woman's face ha ha ha.

Face of a woman as small as my palm
With both eyes I saw it I swear
There were stars I was drunk
Whose wine bar is this ha ha ha.

This is Ali's wine bar this is a table
I show this rope around for no one
Once I was hung in my childhood
Masts were on their ships ha ha ha.

Two sailors filched from Van Gogh
And a woman's face pass out of reach
My whole life I never knew love
Except for Süheyla ha ha ha.

Five o'clock

I raised my hands in Istanbul
Felt a little drunk, amorous, like a minaret
Stopping passers-by
Look I said look how untouched the sky is
And these seagulls look how moody they are
I have five blue eyes
On the thinnest minaret in Istanbul

I put out one of my eyes in Istanbul
Half the fish disappeared
Not a fishtail in sight, I was blind
Once, I'd see women with fans
In their home in their sleep in their husband's arms
A tangle of lips and hair
I'd think how hot they were

On Divanyolu in Istanbul near the sea
I gathered all the passersby in my head
Everyone voiced an opinion
A woman made an excellent job of her silence
I approached and took her hand.
Look I said how moody the seagulls are
And just then the clock struck five

Apple

Stark naked, you're eating an apple now
The apple was a God given apple
One side red the other red too
Birds are flying overhead
Sky is up above
If I remember well it was three days ago you stripped
On top of a wall
On one side red you're eating an apple
On the other hot giving out your love like water
A wall in Istanbul

I'm naked too but I'm not eating an apple
You can't fool me with those apple-tricks
Ohooo I've seen so many apples like that
Birds are flying over my head, these your apple-birds
Sky above me, this your apple-sky
If I remember well we stripped together
Above a church
On one side I'm tolling a bell to grand living
On the other people passing through the street in crowds
A church in a wall

A wall in Istanbul a church in a wall
Stark naked you're eating an apple
You're eating an apple to the sea's core
You're eating an apple to my heart's core
On one side our youth filled with real sorrows
On the other the women of Sirkeci filling trains
Instead of doing their job standing up
Used only to letting their mouths be kissed

I'm dropping one letter from my name*

Translator's note: When C is dropped from Cemal, the remaining letters can
be used to spell "elma', the Turkish word for apple.

Blood Underwrites All Words

Tell me about post vans
Blood underwrites all words
Tell me of Aesop's damned tongue
Blood underwrites all words
Today might be an unexpected day
The lion might stretch out on rocks like a brother
Order tea among rain-scents
Blood underwrites all words
Without reason there you stand
Your voice opened like a fan
An autumn's most cacophonous wing
On the sky's thinnest branch

Blood underwrites all words
Today might be an unexpected day
Saturday might flow like a fountain
Unvoiced consonants in your scream
Are the weight of last night in your veins
How beautifully the street-sellers talks
Bunched together in their felt hats
And the breasts of flower-girls
More guiltless than a swallow's egg
Blood underwrites all words
Here there are no trees to shed leaves
Yet colours might shed all their shades
Your memory works overtime
Among witnessing poets
And actor friends

The journey might seek out a rhyme
In the knot of a horse's tail

Death might seek out a rhyme
In its white shirt

The road looks for a rhyme and finds it
In the likeness of its twists and turns

Blood underwrites all words
Take a rose in hand for instance
Blood underwrites all words
Hold it five minutes before a mirror
Then cut a small piece of that mirror
Inside a piece of white muslin
Place it in your breast pocket
A whole lifetime the mirror smells
Blood underwrites all words
That blood is your smile
It oozed into your life's depths
It's black there it's red
It jumps from branch to branch
It loves the fairytales children are told
But when it comes to defence
It defends only flame
And sun's undying seed
On desolate peaks

Today might be an unexpected for day
Blood underwrites all words

Lakes and Seas

Death?
You're in deep sleep at the bottom of a lake.

Seas?
Gods stir up their depths.

Wine

After twelve
All the drinks
Are wine.

At Just These Times

At just these times water is like an open wound
At the newly opened ends of streets, their tiny ends.
Your sun cistern eyes
Like a broken mirror, like something that shouldn't be
In a house of mourning.
At these times
Like Christ never seen without his cross
We see a man carrying a step ladder
We see a man carrying twelve steps on his back
I love this man so much, this bird too
And how much you love once you love
You upturn the earth with your forehead,
Bowers in the mouths of buildings
Overreach their own confines
Dogs bark at a secret mountain.

All this is good I say they know all about you
Or else how could they know
Their days of exodus spilling from the bucket
Those fish who live on the edge of carbon,
How could miracle-loving Muslims
Enter the house of God
Having hung their coats on the prophet's finger,
And how could the mountain roads be adorned
Where the Greeks buggered goats
During the Return of the Ten Thousand?
Again and then again
Each word we use while making love
Is the burglar's upturned furniture.

Streets bruised blue with minibuses
Where wheat is traded for cash
Where cash is traded for bread
Where bread is traded for tobacco

Where tobacco is traded for pain
And where pain is traded for nothing.
In those streets.
Clocks are showing rain,
Today this little Tuesday
Istanbul lacks everything, apart from hills,
Only Galata
Galata
Slowly slowly feeding to the sea
In the shape of a harmonica
That endless passion for rusting
Nurtured in night's dark cellars.

The Man

A man came across his hat in the street
Who knows whose hat
He did all he could to remember
He remembered a woman white as snow
A woman who opened her windows wide
A woman who knows whose wife
He did all he could to remember.

Stars were heaped on pavements
Because it had rained only shortly before
The man was like a cloud, he remembered
The undersides of his feet
Where stars were real stars
The man walked now on starlight
Because it had rained only moments before

(1953)

Turgut Uyar

One Day, Early in the Morning . . .

Say I knock at the door one day, early morning,
Wake you from your sleep:
And yet, fog still lingers on the Golden Horn.
There's the echo of ferry horns.
Twilight everywhere,
The bridge is still up.
Say I knock at the door early one morning . . .

My journey has been long
The train passed over iron bridges at night.
Villages in the middle of nowhere with five or ten houses.
Telegraph poles all along the route
Running around with us.

Suppose I sang songs from the window,
Woke up, dozed off, woke up again.
My ticket, third class
Poorer than poor.
Say I couldn't buy that meerschaum necklace
So I bought you a basket of apples instead…

Haydarpaşa open your arms we might have said
The ferry glittering at the pier
Air a little cold
Sea smelling of fish and tar
Say I crossed from the bridge to the other shore in a rowing boat,
Climbed our hill in a single breath . . .

Say I knock at the door early one morning,
—Who's that? You'd ask in a sleepy voice.
Your hair ruffled, and heavy-eyed.
Who knows how beautiful you'd look my love,
If I knock at the door one morning,
Wake you from your sleep

And yet, fog still lingers on the Golden Horn.
There's the squeal of factory whistles.

That Village Once More in its Dream

In the mountains of majestic Arsiyan one day
My horse was tired, I was tired.
A stormy, thunderous afternoon
I pulled in the horse's reins, in the rain
Dismounted in Banarhev village . . .

Just me and the Muhtar in his room, two strangers
As though we had known each other for years
We warmed ourselves, drank tea, talked
Of far-off wolves, birds and clouds
And secretly mysteriously I took pleasure
Took pleasure in being human . . .

If a woman's word had come between ours
I'd have felt strange.
In the darkness you wouldn't believe
The distant sounds I heard.
I went to bed, pulled up the quilt
In Banarhev village, in the Muhtar's room
With people and my dreams beside me
I slept until dawn . . .

The heat of the village was in its air.
I know when I went nothing changed.
Let them be happy with their waters, their trout.

. . . .

That village once more in its dream

Evening Dream

Far off ships are passing now
My heart is scattered all over the decks.
Lightened nights, lute sounds, cheese and bread
I've neither ticket nor money nor friend
My heart tremors as I look around
—Turgut wake up, wake up poor one
This is Terme.

Lorries are passing over Terme bridge,
Workmen talk three here, five there
A night begins, half black, half red
I light my cigarette and return home . . .
—Sail on, ships, sail on
Give greetings to wherever you go
Some day far from all worries
I'll come too . . .

Night with Deer

But there was nothing frightening there
Only everything was made of nylon
And when we died we died in thousands against the sun
But before we found the night with deer
We were all afraid like children.

You should all know the night with deer
In far off forests wild and green
Sun sinking slowly over the asphalt road
Redeeming us all from time

First we dug into the earth
And vanished
From gladiators and the cogs of wild machines
From giant cities
Staying hidden and fighting
We saved the night with deer

Yes we were alone but we had hope
If we saw three houses we took it for a city
If we saw three pigeons Mexico came to mind
Evenings we loved to walk the streets
And we loved the way women waited for their husbands
Later we'd drink wine red or white
As soon as we knew it was because of the night with deer

"Behind the night with deer are trees
Sky where its hoof touches water
Cold moonlight on its forked antlers"
Love is remembered whether you want it or not
There were beautiful women and loves in the past
And I know there are now
If only you knew how thinking this pleases me
The most beautiful night with deer in the mountains
Nothing's so important I say
As love and hope
Three glasses and three new songs in an instant
Bristly night with deer lingers in my mind.

I know ships will not convey it
Neon lights and theories will shine no light on its domain
The two of us used to sit and drink for example in Monastir
Or we'd make love in bed a man a woman
Our kisses grew gradually hotter
Our armpits tasted more and more sweetly
In the darkness of the night with deer

But it did not matter that we were deceived
Now that we remembered what everyone else had forgotten
The silver samovars and old things
We loved not simply to reject them
Would you say it was down to our wickedness
We were neither good nor evil
If our situation was different at the beginning and end
Then it's because at the beginning and at the end we were different

But it was the night with deer whatever it was
If you only knew your palms sweated with excitement
We looked on and night descended onto the pavement
Onto crystal chandeliers and naked female shoulders
We felt strange in front of large hotels
Our helplessness was all the easier
If you thought our sadness had great causes you'd be wrong
If we'd drunk three glasses of wine we'd be saved
Or if we'd stabbed a man
Or if we'd spat in the streets
But best of all we'd have gone
Gone to sleep in that night with deer

        "At night the deer's eyes sparkle
        Like distress signals full of fear and confusion
        Like scimitars of sultans in moonlight
        On one side rocks one on top of another
        On the other, me"

But you're miserable so am I
Unconsoled by things grown old
Dominoes and cold afternoons
Crowds of strangers in flowered clothes
Our shadows curled at our feet
We know the end should we ever find pleasure
I forget debts guarantors and bonds
Prizes are drawn without me in this world
At the first sitting I am acquitted
I sit and wash a dark woman for myself
I don't dry her hair well
I drink a glass of wine for myself

        "And yet the night with deer is in the forest
        Sharp blue and rustling
        I pass over into the night with deer"

I stretch out and kiss myself on my cheeks.

Blood Slumber

Only we are beautiful the rest all ugly
And this sweaty darkness too
Then there is something else for sure but I don't know its name
Wherever I start in the end I'm up against that light
Illuminating a brazen half-naked woman's picture
It's evening and I can hardly believe it
Wide-arsed men sit smoking opium
They bake earthen jugs in the sun
So the water they drink is infused with light

I'm afraid of being alone I'm afraid
I work like a horse all day and sleep with women at night

Then the trees look suddenly bigger
Mares have suddenly foaled
The weather is suddenly sun-filled

It's not enough that I've slept with women
I also have to believe that I've slept with them

I don't like it

Trio of Sea-Wavering Blues Reduced to One

A day of deceit and fraud debased not properly lived
An eyeless earless handless footless deficient day
All my failings my darknesses my disorders heaped together
The adventures I've lived these thousand years
These thousand years my darknesses my disorders heaped together
Slowly quietly piled together man on man death on death
So many suns so many water-snakes so many regimes
I give issue to seas and moons disputes and despair
Suddenly I liken blue to someone
Suddenly I recall the mouth of a fish
And I'm cooling off

I've sketched out three places all suitable for you and me
One among sunflowers one at thirty and don't ask about this one
Don't ask about this one I'll tell you someday
When I'm more skilful braver then I'll tell you
First let's lighten this offending darkness
Let's build cities anew like those of today
Let's start again with sesame and bread love affairs and journeys
Let's go and come back
Perhaps in some place in some seed in some state perhaps
Maybe that sound that sip that soft mattress green on greens
I could break stones endlessly shovel dirt pave roads
Chances are we'll be happy let's go and come back
Endlessly I will break stones shovel dirt
Anyway you have thunderous hair like it or not.

The Tailors Came

The tailors came. With things that resembled other huge broken things
On even darker colours and greater fastenings
With things to scare and shame a city.
Fabrics were found and sleeping cats stroked. Then the endless music
                of misery.
There were those who went for tea or to the park late afternoon
Their days shortened conforming to a sorrow that neither increased
                nor diminished . . .
They were tired and pale, they found their fabrics, filled the city
That wreath they brought and carried was a thousand years old,
They'd buried their dead, in great crowds, dust unshaken from them
All the streets were emptied, everyone gave way,

    "Devout women and republicans
    buyers of flowers and sellers of lotteries
    fishermen gathered up their nets and lines
    smokers threw their tabs to the ground and stamped them out."

There was something beneath the unwarmed heavy fabrics, they cut
                and measured
They took out the pattern, compared it,
They cut and measured the end of an unfoldable sleep
And began to sing for a dead horse
Their scissors did not leave their hands
They were expected

    "O horse now dead!—they said—
    How beautiful your madness was, attainable!
    You were open,
    The sole source of thirty thousand breeds!
    Your hair glittering black. Your harness
    —Rubbed and polished with scented oils—

Suited so well your rump and the sky.
Horse, your endless form lent grandeur to the sky
We rubbed your hoofs with palm fibres
And your gallop painted blackness
Awakened all the lands and seas.
We heard your frenzied neighing beside eternity
What beautiful eyes you had, Black horse!
Thousands of people,
—Children, women, men, everyone
In majestic or tatty clothes
The blind and lepers,
The whole crowd of holy books,
Expectant mothers, preachers and sinners
And ice-cream vendors and horse dealers and
Traders and royalists and sailors
Atheists and money lenders
And prophets . . . —
From forests and coasts and barren lands they came
Filled your happy plain
And cried out
You galloped past amid terrific sounds . . ."

The tailors came. Now these suns were outside rooms.
Everyone was trembling and impatient, trembling and impatient in
                    their homes
Newspapers weren't written, we were in the Age of Shops
In hundreds of rooms hundreds of tailors closed their windows
Their slender fingers, pale withered faces yellowing and aging from
                    sitting still
Their broken watch chains, their trembling impatient legs
They approved of the stillness that dominated their lives
They liked it and smiled.

"O horse now dead!—they said—
Your saddle was beautiful
Made of female goatskin, decorated with Orphic gold
It suited the curves of your noble loins
And through you we remembered the beyond.
Others, the sensitivity of beans and beets
The unattainable identity of the cat
On a sunlit roof.
You prompted ships to sail from us
We refreshed your water with giant feasts
You were our festival. Your saddlebags
Were full of coriander and almonds.
Now the world is narrow
Death's great speed has been slowed."

The tailors came. They did not bring fire and blood.
But their sorrows were blood and flame. A whirring thing
Express trains stuck in stations, medicines going crazy
I wandered through the city, not a thing, dusty decanters, shoes
Scattered around all rooms. Dusty decanters, dried up shoes
                    trimmings on the floor,

        "cut-out collars and left-over sleeves
        Cotton padding, diagonal belts, hooks and eyes,
        Buttons, loops
        Pieces of thread and fabric,
        Dark evenings and mornings,
        Shop signs and business cards . . ."

as far as their groins, not even the smallest death.
An impartial love roared over their paleness
They locked up their kitchens, cut huge horse-sized cloths,

"O horse now dead!—they said—
your gallop enlarged the world!
And how you galloped.
We lay down in the south, and you galloped
If there was a beautiful horse, you were more beautiful
With one bright toss your tail divided
And the sky into black
And it was glorious, your fine ornate tail strap.
With the bit in your mouth,
Your bridle made beautiful sounds
And made everyone cried out with joy.
Your head suited our thoughts and
We looked into your eyes with respect . . ."

The tailors came. Their shabby worn out clothes were all dullness
Half-finished. They were never complete. They loved their quarters.
They overcame death with sorrow, worshipped fire.
The city was at their threshold, they felt its wail
They cut, measured, but did not sew or depart,
They threaded the needle's eye and waited;

"O horse now dead!—they said—
O it was the most beautiful, the bond
Between your face and war.
A thorough resistance, balance
And a willing diminution. That much we knew.
That trees were nourished with your blood,
Which nourished us all.
Our puzzlement re-created a country
When we are with you,
Annihilated by your trade, alphabet, pieces of thread
And by daring to put everything straight . . ."

Everyone

Caught unprepared, they had long voices
Long arms and their beards had grown long
Whoever is woken from such a deep sleep
Must surely rub their eyes
Like a black rabbit
In a field of carrots of course
A black rabbit without a carrot
A black-eyed child
Who destroyed Byzantium with Janissaries
And gave his blood to great conquests
A child with forelocks
A child without
With barefooted un-uniformed soldiers
Who never wore glasses
With trussed up crotches
And bread filling their guts
And the pain of death in their hearts
They were caught unprepared

I know an evening like a specimen
Among sounds and expensive flowers
His love befits the sun
And some long gone time
Between certain wheat and barley
Give up darkening my heart
O new soap for God's sake
I walk barefooted
Through water of the wavering paddy field
Most of them remembered old days
And most of them their fathers
Most of them this way and most of them that
They were caught unprepared

Selfish death you can take no one
Some things must remain with us
Things that no one can wear out
A ripe summer evening, a how are you
A how about at dawn
The day turned from Çukurova from the Mediterranean
It turned into a morning festival
Suddenly the water was cut off and evening dragged on
Everyone how nice they were everyone
Was caught unprepared

It Hurts

I want to talk about unhappiness
Vertical and horizontal unhappiness
The perfect unhappiness of the human race
My love hurts

We lived through something full of mystery
They too lived it there
Taking a mountain's crookedness
For its joy

Unhappiness of course first of all
Like a small town bar
Its laughter thumping into daylight
Unreflected here or there
I mean the syphilis someone caught from a wilted rose
The tuberculosis someone else got from a woman
The history of office buildings
The history of promises
My love hurts

Pity my love someone says
Even a child with beautiful eyes
Did not have such a protected summer
I don't know what should be said
My love hurts
Still the ships come and go
Mountains will fade and become clear
And that's all

My air is to find something and enthuse
Autumn has come grief
Winter has come black grief
The cleverest person on the earth
Sometimes in daylight in the middle of summer

My love hurts
Whoever I love
Whoever loves me

Look September gathered up and left
October and the rest will soon be gone
Enormous horses buried in history
Sinking into history that's all

Let's Say You Got Ready

Let's say you got ready for a journey
          "this could be for loneliness too" someone says
let's see are you strong enough
what's your weapon
first asphalt or concrete
then all around you turns suddenly to water
worse still you don't even know how to swim

          "these are the remnants of childhood"
says someone fond of jokes
          "you'll overcome them in any case"
but to know the name of all that I comprehend
suffocates me a little
for example an atomic power project
a jazz concert in Holland
I know I'm going to die in any case
but the sun comes straight towards me
casting my shadow before me
and I confuse my body

actually I'm used to humour but
the fig pierces the rock no matter what
the ship passes over the sea!

Thousands

Thousands of Mondays have passed in my life
I can't recall which it was
I remember eating a cherry with a maggot inside
It must have been fairly old

And also nonsensical things
The back of a girl's knee
A man's ugly style of smoking

How to live in this world of tutelage
Who these lunatics are and how they bare it
It's not my job to unearth anyone's roots
It's enough to sort out my own tale
A beautiful afternoon
Remembering a beautiful old evening
The things filling up
Like demijohns
Swelling my insides

There will be an end I say
But an end to what
To these stone stairs if nothing else

İkinci Yeni

— Biographies & Bibliographies —

Ece Ayhan

(1931–2002)

Born Ece Ayhan Çağlar in the village of Datça, in Muğla province. He was schooled at Atıkalı Elementary School, Zeyrek Secondary School, and Atatürk High School for Boys (1952). He graduated from Ankara University, Faculty of Political Sciences in 1959. He was employed variously as the governor of the provinces of Gürün, Alaca (1962–63), Çardak (1965–66); as a proof-reader and an editor of *Sinematek*, at the Encyclopedia of Meydan Larousse and at *E* Publications, Istanbul. He spent his last days in the care of İzmir Municipality at the Gürçeşme Rest Home, where he died on 12 July 2002. He is buried in the village Yalova in Eceabat, Çanakkale.

Poetry: *Kınar Hanım'ın Denizleri* (Kınar Hanim's Seas, 1959), *Bakışsız Bir Kedi Kara* (A Faceless Cat Black, 1965), *Ortodoksluklar* (Orthodoxies, 1968), *Devlet ve Tabiat ya da Orta İkiden Ayrılan Çocuklar İçin Şiirler* (State and Nature or Poems for Children Leaving School in Seventh Grade, 1973), *Yort Savul* (Yort Savul, 1977), *Zambaklı Padişah* (Sultan with a Lily, 1981), *Çok Eski Adıyladır* (With His Ancient Name, 1982), *Çanakkaleli Melahat'a İki El Mektup ya da Özel Bir Fuhuş Tarihi* (Two Letters to Melahat of Çanakkale or A Private History of Prostitution, 1991), *Son Şiirler* (Last Poems, 1993), *Sivil Şiirler* (Civilian Poems, 1993), *Bütün Yort Savullar* (Collected Poems, 1994).

Interviews: *Hay Hak! Söyleşiler!* (Oh My God! Interviews!, 2002).

Other Works: *Defterler* (Notebooks, 1981), *Yalnız Kardeşçe* (Brotherly Only, interview, 1984), *Kolsuz Bir Hattat* (An Armless Calligrapher,1987), *Şiirin Bir Altın Çağı* (A Golden Age of Poetry, 1993), *Aynalı Denemeler ya da Yalınayak Bir Türkçeyledir* (Essays with a Mirror or In Barefoot Turkish, 1995), *Dipyazılar* (Footnotes, 1996), *Morötesi Requiem Ağzıbozuk Bir Minyatür* (Ultraviolet Requiem A Swearing Miniature, 1997), *Sivil Denemeler Kara* (Civilian Essays Black, 1998), *Bir Şiirin Bakır Çağı* (Copper Age of a Poem, 2002).

In English: *A Blind Cat Black & Orthodoxies* (Sun & Moon, Los Angeles, 1997).

İlhan Berk
(1918–2008)

Born İlhan Nurullah Berk, in Manisa. He graduated from Necati Bey Teacher Training College and worked for some time as a teacher in Giresun. He later graduated from Ankara Gazi Institute of Education, Department of French in 1945. He worked as a secondary school teacher in Zonguldak, Samsun and Kırşehir from 1945 to 1955. He was a translator in the publications office of the General Directorate of Ziraat Bank from 1956 until his retirement in 1969. Berk lived in the Aegean town of Bodrum where he died on August 28, 2008.

Poetry: *Güneşi Yakanların Selamı* (Salute of The Sun Burners, 1935), *İstanbul* (İstanbul, 1947), *Günaydın Yeryüzü* (Good Morning Earth, 1952), *Türkiye Şarkısı* (Song of Turkey, 1953), *Köroğlu* (Köroğlu, 1955), *Galile Denizi* (The Sea of Galilee, 1958), *Çivi Yazısı* (Cuneiform Writing, 1960), *Otağ* (The Royal Tent, 1961), *Mısırkalyoniğne* (Corn-galley-needle, 1962), *Aşıkane* (Amorously, 1968), *Şenlikname* (Letter of Joy, 1972), *Şiirler* (Poems, 1975), *Taş Baskısı* (Lithograph, 1975), *Atlas* (Atlas, 1975, 87), *Kül* (Ash, 1978), *İstanbul Kitabı* (The Book of İstanbul, 1979), *Kitaplar Kitabı* (Book of Books, 1981), *Şifalı Otlar Kitabı* (The Book of Healing Herbs, 1982), *Deniz Eskisi* (The Age of the Sea, published with *Şiirin Gizli Tarihi* -The Secret History of Poetry, 1982), *Günaydın Yeryüzü* (Good Morning Earth, 1982), *Galata* (Galata, 1983), *Delta ve Çocuk* (Delta and Child, 1984), *Güzel Irmak* (Beautiful River, published with *Şairin Kanı* - Blood of the Poet, 1988), *Pera* (Pera, 1990), *Dün Dağlarda Dolaştım Evde Yoktum* (Yesterday I wasn't at Home, I Took to the Hills, 1993), *Avluya Düşen Gölge* (Shadow Fallen Across the Courtyard, 1998), *Çok Yaşasın Sayılar* (Long Live Numbers, 1998), *Kült Kitap* (Cult, 1999), *Şeyler Kitabı* (The Book of Things, 2002), *Requiem* (2004), *Kuşların Doğum Gününde Olacağım* (I'll be at the Bird's Birthday, 2005), *Adlandırılmayan Yoktur—Aforizmalar* (Aphorisms, 2006).

Anthologies: *Başlangıcından Bugüne Beyit Mısra Antolojisi* (An Anthology of Couplets from the Beginning until Today, 1960), *Rimbaud'un Seçme Şiirleri* (Selected Poems of Arthur Rimbaud, 1982), *Aşk Şiirleri* (Love Poems, 1965), *Dünya Edebiyatından Aşk Şiirleri* (Love Poems from World Literature, 1968), *Dünya Şiiri* (World Poetry, 1969).

Autobiography: *Bir Uzun Adam* (A Tall Man, 1982).

Journals: *El Yazılarına Vuruyor Güneş: 1955-1990* (The Sun Beats Down on Your Manuscripts, 1983; expanded edition, 1992), *İnferno* (Inferno, 1995).

Essays: *Şiirin Açık Tarihi* (The Open History of Poetry, 1984), *Şairin Toprağı* (The Poet's Turf, 1992), *Logos* (Logos, 1996), *Poetika* (Poetics, 1997).

Interviews: *Kanatlı At* (The Winged Horse, 1994).

In English: *A Leaf About to Fall: Selected Poems* (Salt Publishing, Cambridge, 2006), *Madrigals* (Shearsman Books, Exeter, 2008), *The Book of Things* (Salt Publishing, 2009).

Edip Cansever
(1928–1986)

Cansever was born on 9 August 1928 in Istanbul. After completing his education at the Istanbul High School for Boys in 1946, he entered the High School of Trade and shortly thereafter went to work for his father in the Grand Bazaar. After a posting in Ankara for military service, he opened his own antique shop in 1950, also in Istanbul's Grand Bazaar, where he worked until his retirement in 1975. He died from severe gastric bleeding brought on by cirrhosis on 28 May 1986.

Poetry: *İkindi Üstü* (Late Afternoon, 1947), *Dirlik Düzenlik* (Unity and Order, 1954), *Yerçekimli Karanfil* (Gravitational Carnation, 1957), *Umutsuzlar Parkı* (Park of Hopelessness, 1958), *Petrol* (Petroleum, 1959), *Nerde Antigone* (Where is Antigone, 1961), *Tragedyalar* (Tragedies, 1964), *Çağrılmayan Yakup* (Yakup Uninvited, 1969), *Kirli Ağustos* (Dirty August, 1970), *Sonrası Kalır* (The Rest Remains, 1974), *Ben Ruhi Bey Nasılım* (I'm Ruhi Bey How am I, 1976), *Sevda ile Sevi* (Love and Affection, 1977), *Şairin Seyir Defteri* (Poet's Logbook, 1980), *Yeniden* (Again, 1981), *Bezik Oynayan Kadınlar* (Women Bezique Players, 1982), *İlkyaz Şikâyetçileri* (Spring Mouners, 1982), *Oteller Kenti* (City of Hotels, 1985), *Gün Dönüyor Avucumda* (Sun Revolves in My Palm, 1987), *Karanfil Elden Ele* (Carnation from Hand to Hand, 2002).

In English: *Dirty August: Selected Poems* (Talisman House, Jersey City, NJ, 2010).

Cemal Süreya
(1931–1990)

Born in the Eastern Turkish city of Erzincan in 1931, his real name was Cemalettin Seber. Some of his many pen names were Adil Fırat, Ali Fakir, Birsen Sağanak, Dr. Suat Hüseyin, Hasan Basri, Genco Gümrah, Osman Mazlum and Suna Gün. He graduated from Haydarpaşa High School in 1950 and Ankara University's Faculty of Political Sciences, Department of Public Finance in 1954. He worked as an assistant and inspector at the Ministry of Finance. After an interval of some years, he resumed his office as inspector in 1971 and retired as an advisor in 1982. From 1975 to 1976, he served as member of the Financial Inspection Board, Director of the Mint. In 1978, he became a member of the consultative board of the Ministry of Culture.

Süreya was also a prolific newspaper columnist and political commentator. A poetry award has been held in his name since 9 January 1990.

Poetry: *Üvercinka* (Pigeon-Tongued, 1958), *Göçebe* (Nomad, 1965), *Beni Öp Sonra Doğur Beni* (Kiss Me Then Give Birth to Me, 1973), *Sevda Sözleri* (Words of Love, 1984), *Güz Bitiği* (Autumn's End, 1988), *Sıcak Nal* (Warm Horseshoe, 1988).

Essays: *Şapkam Dolu Çiçekle* (My Hat Full of Flowers, 1976), *Günübirlik* (Overnight, 1982), *Onüç Günün Mektupları* (Thirteen Day Letters, 1990), *99 Yüz* (99 Faces, 1991), *999. Gün / Üstü Kalsın* (999th Day / Keep the Change, 1991), *Folklor Şiire Düşman* (Folklore is the Enemy of Poetry, 1992), *Uzat Saçlarını Frigya* (Grow Your Hair Long, Phrygia, 1992), *Aydınlık Yazıları / Paçal* (Articles of Illumination, 1992), *Oluşum'da Cemal Süreya* (Cemal Süreya in Oluşum, 1992), *Papirüs'ten Başyazılar* (Editorials from Papirüs, 1992), *Günler* (Days, 1996), *Güvercin Curnatası* (Pigeons' Rosemary - conversations, 1997), *Soluğundan Öptüm Seni* (I Kissed You on Your Breath, 2003).

Anthologies: *Mülkiyeli Şairler* (Poets of Civil Society, 1966), *100 Aşk Şiiri* (100 Love Poems, 1967).

Children's Literature: *Aritmetik İyi Kuşlar Pek İyi* (Arithmetic Good, Birds Very Good, 1993).

Turgut Uyar
(1927–1985)

Uyar was born in Ankara in 1927. He graduated from Bursa Military High School in 1946 and the Military Officers School in 1947. His first army posting was to Posof. Afterwards, he was appointed to the Draft Office in Terme and then to Ankara.

He resigned his military commission in 1958 and started work at the Ankara bureau of the Turkish Cellulose and Paper Factories Corporation. He moved permanently to Istanbul following his retirement in 1969. In the same year he married the writer Tomris Uyar. In later years Uyar's health gave way under the weight of his alcohol addiction. He died on 22 August 1985 in Istanbul.

Uyar won many awards, including the 1963 Yeditepe Poetry Prize for *Tütünler Islak* (The Tobacco is Wet, 1962), the 1982 Behçet Necatigil Poetry Award for *Kayayı Delen İncir* (The Fig That Pierces Stone) and the 1984 Sedat Simavi Foundation Literature Award for *Büyük Saat* (The Great Clock, 1981).

Poetry: *Arz-ı Hal* (Petition, 1949), *Türkiyem* (My Turkey, 1952), *Dünyanın En Güzel Arabistanı* (The World's Most Beautiful Arabia, 1959), *Tütünler Islak* (The Tobacco is Wet, 1962), *Her Pazartesi* (Every Monday, 1968), *Divan* (Divan, 1970), *Toplandılar* (They Gathered, 1974), *Kayayı Delen İncir* (The Fig That Pierces Stone, 1981), *Büyük Saat / Bütün Şiirleri* (The Great Clock / Collected Poems, 1981), *Dün Yok mu?* (Was There No Yesterday?, 1984), *Sonsuz ve Öbürü* (Eternity and the Next, 1985), *Bütün Şiirleri* (Collected Poems, in 3 volumes, 1994).

Essays: *Bir Şiirden* (From a Poem, 1983).